CLASS   MYTHS

and   culture

CLASS MYTHS

and culture
by
Stefan Szczelkun.

1990

WORKING PRESS

books by and about

working class artists

CLASS MYTHS & culture
Stefan Szczelkun

WORKING PRESS
books by and about working class artists

Copyright Stefan Szczelkun 1990

Published by Working Press, 85 St Agnes Place,
Kennington, London SE11 4BB

Typesetting by Counter Productions,
PO Box 556 London SE5 0RL

Printed by Antony Rowe Ltd,
Chippenham, Wiltshire

Cover photos by Patrick Gilbert

British Library Cataloguing in Publication Data
Szczelkun, Stefan 1948-
Class Myth & culture
1. Social Class. Cultural aspects
I. Title
305.5

ISBN 1-870736-03-6

dedicated to Lech

CONTENTS

MYTHS OF CLASS IDENTITY

There is much confusion around today about class. Many people do not feel comfortable with any class identity and feel they therefore must be 'classless'. Many others who do not fit the traditional image of working class, who have had an education or acquired property, feel they must be middle or lower-middle class. I'd like to talk about class oppression and especially how it affects these groups from the viewpoint of my own history.

I see class identity as not only related to an economic position but also as a matter of culture and heritage. (Culture being the sum total of a particular peoples activity characterised by language, custom, ritual, art, sport, attitudes and so on). One of the original oppressive stereotypes of working people was that they were 'without culture'. Another myth, that has become prominent more recently, is that they have 'a' culture but without much depth or lasting value. In fact working people comprise the majority of the population and have many cultures which vary regionally,

1

ethnically and in other ways. It is a supremacist assumption that one culture can be compared as better or worse than another.

An important characteristic of the modern working class is this diversity. And yet we are still stuck with a ridiculous cloth cap image of the working class as a homogenous minority group which has had its day and is now a minority in decline.

* * *

My Great Grandad Smith was a coalmine foreman in Nottingham. Of his ten children at least his son Sidney felt he was a cut above the ordinary proletarian. Sidney survived in the general strike of 1926 by selling potatoes grown on two allottments off his bike. After the failure of the general strike he became disillusioned with the organised working class and determined never to go back down the mines. He managed to set up a business selling vegetables from a lorry which he later expanded into the garage behind his house on the Derby road. Next door in the papershop was the young Brian Clough. Ambition was in the air. "Make something of yourself" was the catch phrase.

Great Granny Johnson was a giant of a woman who, after her lay preacher husband met an early death, brought up ten children on her own by working in the fields. They lived for some years in a scruffily thatched little two room mud walled 'cottage' in Little Lunnon (now a ploughed field) where they survived the winter by gleaning and keeping a pig. Daisy, the eldest daughter, after some years of taking the baby into school with her, was expected to go into service to help support the family. As pastry cook in an entourage of 25 servants she waited on two nobs in Upsley Castle in Yorkshire. In all she was in service for over 15 years and got a taste for the more moral and savoury upper class mores. Finally she met and married Sidney Smith.

Sidney listened to all the woes of his customers. He probably then expressed his feelings of contempt for their helplessness to his only daughter.

My mother Joan had to find a way to continue this effort at bettering herself. The amount of middle class doctors willing to marry even a pretty working class nurse was to say the least limited. She solved the problem in her own way, taking advantage of the flux of war, by choosing a handsome long haired Polish Pilot. Sidney was shocked .... a foreigner!

Walerian's father had been a signalman on the railway in eastern Poland. They lived in a little log house by a lake in a pretty peasant village called Glenbokie. I know little about his mother. I never met them, as they survived the war but died before we managed to return to Poland in the '60s. His village school must have been progessive and he had just gone to study engineering in Warsaw when the war broke. After surviving a harsh period in a Russian concentration camp he made his way to England and joined the RAF as a Mosquito pilot. After the war he got a job as a draughtsman in the expanding aerospace industry.

The mood in England was of conditional and wary acceptance. 'Aliens' were acceptable as long as they did not expect to be welcomed with their foreign ways. The expectation was that you gave up any public expression of your ethnic identity as quickly as possible. The only other possibility was to live in a ghetto with your own people. Assimilation was clearly a safer choice if you could take it. On top of this, Walerian couldn't return to Poland to reinforce his family's connection to his culture. It was dangerous to return in those days without first gaining British citizenship. He may not have been allowed to leave, or at worst may have been interned. Glenbokie itself had become part of the USSR and was inaccessible. In his effort to become Anglicised he thought it would only be a burden for us to be taught Polish... better if we were brought up 'English'. So Polish language and culture for me was simply overheard at Sunday dinner with Polish friends. The fear behind this denial of my dads first language to his beloved son must have been apparent to me. At the same time my dad, the second closest person to me, was Polish in every bit of his being. Even his adopted Englishnesses were Polish. I became Polish on a very subtle and intimate level.

Meanwhile my mother was also busy adopting a new way of speaking, dropping the Nottinghamshire dialect for a posher London voice. She became a housewife and mother. Her powerful drive to get somewhere was channelled through her house and children.

My argumentative brightness had always contrasted with an erratic academic record in local state schools. As it was I managed to scrape two A levels. I wanted to do art and science but the school only allowed one or the other so I did science. Joan wanted me to be a doctor, the prime symbol of humanitarian respectability. I wanted to be an artist. The realistic compromise was architecture, which appealed to me with its promised fusion of art and science. I went to Portsmouth Polytechnic, a relatively new institution which allowed thousands of lower-class young people to get a higher education for the first time. Away from home a blurred perspective on my own situation slowly developed. Underlying architectural education was a subtext of learning how to behave in a professional manner. This meant giving off an air of superior knowledge and distancing oneself from the other workers in the building industry. Behind the Bauhaus idealism and the Design Method rationalism class division was the base line. I found it impossible to accept a designated role as an architect.

If it had been simply a matter of acquiring more money or even more human work conditions that motivated us things may have been more straightforward. But the move to better oneself was in direct reaction to the definition of working class people that was disseminated from above. Peoples desperate behaviour in the face of economic exploitation had long been used as an illustration of the inherent nature of working class people. According to the ruling class it was not the conditions they endured that made them appear to be like this but their own base natures (which then justified the brutal exploitation.) At the same time the owning class defined human beings in terms of their own image. People who didn't match this description were treated as lesser mortals.

This vile myth was put across with all the force of upper & middle class power (Literary monopoly etc.) It was persuasive. Working people were shamed and humiliated. Not only were they exploited to a truly degrading extent but were then told that they had brought these conditions upon themselves and got nothing more than they deserved as inferior beings.

The details of this definition were a catalogue of

inhumanity, the enormity of which it seems too painful to picture. Working Class people were made to appear to be inately worth less and worthless, stupid, dirty, smelly, brutish, deficient, untrustworthy, evil, ill mannered, uncultured, unsophisticated, uncouth, badly spoken and lacking most characteristics that distinguish humans from animals. They were in fact reduced to the status of clever animals. From now on I will call this 'The Definition'. These negative words came to characterise the working class.

Owning-class culture had many achievements to admire: fine clothes, carriages, architecture, books, opera, symphonies, oil paintings and so on. The taking of surplus value from working people in the form of profits led to much time being put into the pursuit of culture. (Of course much of this culture was produced by the skill of more workers.) However, there were characteristics of owning-class behaviour that were rigid and less than admirable. For instance, the pretence, the restraint, the lack of physicality & the emotional self-control. These were ruling-class norms, the standards of propriety and cultured behaviour. If any person should act otherwise it was a sign of vulgarity. Raucus, lively, physical and spontaneous behaviour associated with the working classes was bad. Discipline, order and stiffness was good. (Giving rise to phrases like 'stiff upper lip' and 'stuck up'.) In this way even natural exuberance and emotional openness came to indicate a similarity with animals. Self-control was seen as a central civilising concept and something that the working classes lacked.

So the Definition was believed to a greater or lesser extent by working class people. It gave us a fatalistic attitude to our suffering. We internalised the oppression and expected nothing more. It gave us a negative identity and self image.

The overall effect is hopelessness and powerlessness. The current inheritance of this attitude is the ubiquitous myth that to think that it is possible to end class society now is laughable and that class as an issue is passe. I am told that we now have a society of 'haves' (ie houseowners) who out-vote the 'have nots' (council tenants and the third world) and that the best that can be achieved, stretching our meagre and perished imagination to its limit, is that the haves show a bit of concern for the have nots. The empty humour of Comic Relief and the elastoplast approach to world hunger that is Band Aid.

How different it would feel if we had been brought up with a true picture of working-class people as couragous, quick witted, resourceful, perservering, honest, generous, clear thinking, direct, relaxed, funny, concerned, bold and so on...

Apart from those who were destroyed or numbed out by the Definition and by exploitation there were two possible attitudes to take. Fight or flight.

The first saw that the Definition was false. These people organised workers and formed the socialist, communist and anarchist movements or simply resisted in their own way by sabotage and various forms of non-participation. These organisations achieved massive improvements, especially in education and health. Unfortunately essential information about how the exploitation and the Definition had actually hurt people and made them powerless was lacking. The internalised stereotypes continued to afflict people even when they were active in the Labour Party or other workers' organisations. There was no understanding about how the damage done by oppression was a hurt that could be systematically undone or healed. This seriously limited the capacity of the numerous workers organisations to get to the root of oppression.

Educational reform and mass welfare did in fact change a lot more than is evident. The fact that the validity of the Definition was denied was important; and probably led to a limited intuitive resolution of this damage. Unfortunately the radical implication of the expansion of higher education has been disguised by a myth which dubs all educated working class people as middle class. By definition working class people are not intelligent so if you've got a degree you must be middle class. This nonsense is reinforced by the fact that academic traditions are laden with class assumptions and are presented in upper class styles even in the Polytechnics. This has created much confusion.

The Definition was therefore largely passed on to new generations who may not themselves have actualy suffered the same rigours of exploitation (in that they have not, in most cases, had to struggle to survive physically). The 'fight' strategy denied the definition to some extent but the struggle to improve overall conditions was frustratingly slow. There were a few ways that working class men could get rich quick, but they were limited. Most of the better paid and higher status professions were barred to people who did not display the correct behaviour. Working class culture was spurned in all its manifestations. Few if any doctors or university professors spoke with a strong dialect for instance. A secretary coming to London from Birmingham would not get a job answering the telephone. . . unless. . .

The other way out was by changing your behaviour to the extent that one took on a new more acceptable identity. An identity that left out what was bad and affected what was good. In this way it was thought the Definition wouldn't stick any more, the crushing effect of negative images of yourself would be lifted and many higher status jobs and power positions in the expanding consumer society would become accesible.

* * *

The Middle Class Veneer: By imitating manners, speech patterns and cultural standards of the ruling classes and by suppressing the wide regional and ethnic immigrant variety of working class cultural traits, people would get their ticket to respectability.

For lower middle class people the idea of good judgement was the key. Good judgement is not the absolute that it seems to be but simple adherence to the complex and subtle middle class rules of taste. It is crucial that aspiring lower middle class people get this right. Their sense of identity and self-worth depends on it. For the real middle class, their identity is made secure by wealth. They can hire a top interior designer. Whereas LMCs must D.I.Y. LMCs distinguish themselves from common people by their sense of good taste. Without it their self esteem evaporates.

However, this path did not contradict the oppression but in fact reinforced its claim to be truth. In effect this means that people had accepted the massively hurtful Definition as true; but by starting an apparently new life, they attempted to leave it behind. Unfortunately, the unresolved hurt stayed with them in their

bodies and found its expression in depression, despera-
tion and disease, souring and disturbing their inner
functioning and human relationships.

A friend's report: "It is only now that I am realising
the full pyschological horror of my own experience as a
child. Every bit of behaviour and appearance was
under constant surveillance and criticism. For the first
seven years of my life I was an only child... My natural
tendency to adapt to my working class social surround-
ings was interrupted with all types of imposed controls
and coercions. When I grew out of physical intimidation
I was controlled economically. The development of my
own judgement was under constant attack. My mother
was always there interfering with all aspects of my life.
Mealtimes were dominated by a regime of table manners which we seemed to eternally resist although it
resulted in mealtime misery. Without this constant
control she feared we would eat like pigs. Convinced
she was doing the best for us she was in fact systematically destroying the children she loved so dearly."

Daily life was a battle ground of class warfare.
Mother as an unwitting and tragic agent of class oppression. A normal family.

The contradictions within their crude imitation of
middle class culture were jarring and discordant.
Sometimes this took the form of simply a hotch potch of
linguistic usuage and conventions made more complex
for me by my dads mixture of English words with Polish
grammer and accent. At other times they were glaring
absurdities. In our family Sidney owned the first book
ever. A compilation of Bubbles magazines with colour
pictures. As I grew up my connection to the middle/c
literary tradition (lynch pin of bourgeoise culture) was

via Readers Digest and Illustrated Classics. A major structural element of this cultural identity that we were meant to be assuming was just not there. The oral tradition was still the underlying structure to our thinking.

The effects of this self imposed social engineering have left me with profound patterns of isolation which I am only now unravelling 20 years later.

The new veneer of respectability does not add up to a successful Culture. It is too derivative, contradictory, imitative, based on hearsay, too false to function. A culture is organically derived, built up, layered, interconnected, complex, it has an integrity and depth. This Lower middle class stuff is empty, vacuous, a pretense, a charade. Respectability is an artificial construct, too brittle and transparent to support human life. The chasms that open up are filled with endless TV spectaculars and commodity dreaming. Glamorous illusions like the deserted Shepperton film sets I used to play in as a boy.

But under our surface behaviour old working class cultural forms still exist, their voices muted, rumbling, omniscient. Occasionally sprouting through cracks in the concrete.

To further add to the confusion there are, amongst these ranks of the displaced, the downwardly mobile ex-middle-class still clinging pitfully to their pretentious 'values.' It is the Definition which does not let them relaxedly integrate and become the working class people they surely now are.

I have been amazed by the panic stricken and violent attitude of middle class people towards their own young who appear not to be showing intellectual prowess. 'A good education' is equated with survival.

* * *

Commercial Culture: and its attendant media, in a market response to these myths, reinforced and exaggerated the illusions of respectable culture. I grew up in this ersatz non culture. A badly made glamorous collage of a culture that didn't fit together. Media myth modelling focused on two areas.

Appearance was one. We had arisen from the proletarian dirt and disease... we were the beautiful people. It was known that certain of the working classes could escape to become stars. If you were exceptionally beautiful. We hoped our noses would stay youthfully small. Hands cultured and manicured; slim artistic fingers were to be valued. We chewed our nails in anguish. The media bombarded us with impossible goals of glamour. Cleanliness was next to Godliness. The myths of hygiene enforced with soap are worth a book in themselves. The human skin was the prime target and canvas on which this new human was to be described. We lived in such a frightening and unreal world, terrorised by blackheads and dandruff.

Language was the next target. There was simply a right and a wrong way to speak and spell. Punishment was due those who made their own decisions. There was imminent danger of a slide back into the morass; a slip of the tongue was enough.

"Ain't it lovely, mum." SLAP!. "ISN'T IT lovely. Not ain't. We won't have that slovenly speech in this house." And it wasn't allowed on TV either except as an object of derision. Can you imagine a BBC newreader with a broad Nottingham or Polish accent?

At school we were again forcefully reminded of the correct language in which to communicate. And the exclusion of those who did not speak and write it was manifest by the division into separate institutions at the age of 11. In addition it must be noted that in my 13 years of schooling there was never the slightest acknowledgement of my Polish background.

We were to be the storm troops of respectability to be disciplined at all costs. Our 'animal natures' were to be trained out of us. This was our chance to pull our socks up and become human beings instead of trash. Knowledge was equated with intelligence. ...Why did we resist so and drive the well meaning teachers wild with exasperation?

The charade once started gathered momentum. It has built up a monumental artifice that does not nurture human life and has effectively passed on to us the dead heritage of the Definition..

* * *

Youth Culture: Apart from individual resistance at home and at school there was an intuitive cultural resistance to this imposed culture within which we felt imprisoned. As youth our reps The Who screamed 'Talkin bout my generation' and we made up mod, hip, punk, culture in desperate attempts to make our own new culture or find an expression for this abstact torment that we felt. In fact we produced new inverted myths of superiority.

But still perhaps we did the best at adaption in a situation which was more difficult than it appeared at the time. If we could have healed that dead space in our minds left by the unresolved hurt of the Definition things might have been different. As it was the commercial context soon sucked these sub-cultural revolts dry.

I do not mean to imply that traditional working class cultures were all good. They are very restrictive and prescriptive. Often damaged and rigidified by the ravages of past or present oppressors. We need to be critical of tradition but savour what is good.

We need a culture of depth, structural integrity and connection that is also spontaneous, flexible and a conscious choice. A nurturing culture which includes the methods and techniques to heal these deep hurts of the past as daily practices. A culture of constant vociferous outrage at the rape of our earth and its peoples. A culture that respects young people and gives them a positive self image.

I think I have taken what is most human out of this disaster. The working class achievement of the welfare state and education has given me free time. Sidney would have have dissapproved but one of the justifications offered for the class exploitation of other human beings was to achieve free time and resources to reflect and BE CREATIVE was it not? During the 19C much of the working class struggle was for the achievement of free time, weekends, holidays. So in this way I think I have achieved their ambitions in denying wage slavery and defining the use of my own time almost entirely. This has not been easy because my assumptions have been at variance with the traditions and style of the reflective class.

I'd like to catalogue all the ways in which oppression works on us. To make working drawings of its construction so that we can begin to dismantle it. Invisible though it is, it has no more claim to existence than a torture machine covered in barbs and chains. But because an effect of all hurt is to shut down flexible thinking it is a huge area cordoned off in the minds of EVERYONE.

The lower middling classes, although they have clawed material advantages from capitalisms rape of the earth, are still a classically exploited class. In fact they are still wage workers or families of wage workers who have taken on the appearance of respectability in order to get on. But still a part of the value that they produce is creamed off by an owning class who largely direct the world to their own callous advantage.

Lower middle class culture is nothing but a shroud that covers a festering corpse of self loathing. A lie that poisons the spirit and our love and passion for those around us. A self hatred which becomes manifest in all sorts of horrid diseases and self immolation on the spike of alcohol and drugs.

Protected by a moat of repressed tears the outrage of class oppression all around us goes unchallenged.

What I'm suggesting is that this historically new lower or pseudo middle class, contrary to the myth which suggests that because we have achieved privileges everything must be OK, is another extremely vicious form of class oppression, the pressures of which can destroy body, mind and spirit. We have yet to uncover and repair the massive injury done to ourselves by the Definition and our attempts to survive it. An important early step in this process is the uncovering and telling of our own life stories. Telling them in a way that allows us to feel and express how bad it was and also to celebrate our resistance and survival and the gains we have made.

ARTISTS' LIBERATION

The ability to make something new, the main or only function is the quality of its own existence, is profoundly and uniquely human. The awareness of the quality of our lives is tied up with this activity and its products.

Although all humans have this ability at present it is only a small number who dedicate their working lives to this activity. These people are called artists. What they engage in is what I am defining broadly as art.

Artists produce value. However they are rarely adequately recompensed for this work even tho' large amounts of money are exchanged for works of art. The great art that is the focus of the art market would not have been produced without the whole community of artists. Even the artists who produced 'great art' often got only a tiny portion of the value they produced whilst they were alive. After they died the value of their work would rise astronomically but none of this value would find its way back to artists.

Artists clearly work and are exploited. We can

fairly say that all artists are in a class of workers from this economic standpoint.

Artists hold onto an important human ideal of freedom. That is the freedom to produce exactly what you decide to in exactly the way you want. This is in stark contrast with the lot of most wage workers who are told what to produce or who produce to satisfy market demands. Of course many artists produce to satisfy market demands as well. But the artists that hold on to this ideal hold out a model of the liberated worker who has control over the hours she works and what s/he produces. This is anathema to the coercive and mechanistic nature of capitalism.

The result of this is that artists are usually not paid to go about their business. They have to find other work to support their vocation. The only group of workers who share this outright refusal to recognise their work as valid production are parents.

Exploitation is only maintained by oppression. Oppression is the systematic hurts imposed on people by society. As well as the generalised oppressions of broad classes in society each sub group of workers will suffer from specific oppression directed at their particular situation. Artists are invalidated as lazy dropouts, dreamers, idealists, social parasites, weird, temperamental, mad geniuses, inspired by hardship and suffering, heroes, specially gifted, privileged.

Artists particularly feel pressure from rigid societal concepts of 'normal behaviour'. Fear of repression from the mental health system makes people keep within conservative norms of behaviour. Norms of behaviour which are not necessarily conducive to creativity amongst other things.

Because of this vicious oppression artists are often radicals and progressives. However they have not been so good at standing up against their own oppression. This has not been helped by the fact that the broad workers' movement has not been a good ally for artists whose demand to determine their own productive goals is in some respects too radical. (And this is where the privilege myth sticks) In fact artists are often attacked. In a recent pamphlet I noticed this ; "London transports main attempt to 'improve' matters appears to be a campaign of colourful posters extolling the wonders of the tube system and featuring a series of specially commisioned paintings.(Once again artists, those specialists of creativity, are exposed as the vanguard of marketing, selling us a way of life that denies the real creative powers of the rest of us)." Red Menace, October 1989. How they imagine that it is artists that "deny the real creative powers of the rest of us." is beyond logic but does show the depth of resentment around that is misdirected at artists by the oppressive myths which again set one group of workers against another.

The 'solitary activity' of the artist (a stereotype rather than a necessary reality) has played against the formation of a strong artists organisation. In fact artists are so hurt by the oppression that they tend to believe many of the stereotypes and myths about themselves and take role identities based on them. ARTISTS HOWEVER NEED TO BE ORGANISED AND THEY NEED TO FIND FORMAL ALLIES IF THEIR LIVES ARE TO IMPROVE.

This organisation will be best made from many smaller groups of artists who meet for mutual support and validation around shared interests. The deeper these 'interests', the more chance of the group persisting and gaining strength. For instance a group with the identity of 'working class women artists' will find more satisfaction in meeting than oil painters or people sharing studio premises. It is essential that artists meet around these very specific issues of identity, and work out their own needs and how oppression has acted on each of their lives before meeting broadly as artists. Without this recognition of diversity a broad-based artists' organisation will not function for long with much enthusiasm from the membership.

If artists are united they do have economic clout. They can change the policies of those organisations on whom they rely. The National Artists Association has achieved much in spite of its lack of liberation policy and correct organisation.

There is no real shortage of resources to support art activity. There is only an illusion of scarcity. Artists are humiliated by being forced to compete for a few crumbs when the value they have produced in recent history alone could make each artist well paid. People will welcome art in their lives if artists adopt policies of liberation rather than being passively used, by their silence, to bolster the status quo. There cannot be 'too much art'.

At the same time it is clear that artists cannot be entirely liberated until class society as a whole is overcome. Artists Liberation is an important element of this major step in human evolution.

The New Working Class
Intelligentsia

The expansion of higher education into the post-war years in Britain was followed by the entry of many thousands of upwardly (and not so upwardly) mobile working class youth from the poorer state grammer schools into the new Polytechnics and Art Schools. For the first time ever a large but INVISIBLE working class intelligentsia has been created.

It is invisible and almost unconcious because in British terms a working class intelligentsia is impossible: by definition the working classes are 'not intelligent'. People processed by higher education are supposed, magically, to become middle class. Of course the curriculum and expected mannerisms, style, language, accent and so on are all firmly derived from middle class academic tradition. But it is absurd to expect a few years of higher education to change one's identity even with a bit of preparation from ambitious parents keen for their children to get on and better themselves. Class identity goes a lot deeper than learning facts or manners. Taking your elbows off the table and learning to say thingy rather than fingy don't, sorry doesn't, make you middle class any more than being on a monthly wage, wearing a white collar or owning your own house...

In the fab sixties the first wave from the lower echelons of society started to make trouble and demand in a loud and naive way a social relevance to art practice. This huge struggle resulted in a whole new category being created to contain and defuse them.

COMMUNITY ART was born to protect Fine Art from the riff raff. Community artists, for all their achievements were instantly relegated to the fourth division in the league of Status and Meaning.

For the first time in history a large section of the population is trying to realise their vocation in Art. Along with the college grant aid scheme and unemployment benefit the result is a huge number of artists who have no place in society but continue to work without pay and sometimes even without exposure.

If all these common yobs have gone to art college, you may ask, where are they now ? Why aren't they causing a stink ?

The discomfort with fine art practice (and FAs intolerance of them) has lead them into other categories of art practice which both allow them to survive and, sometimes even find more space for their expressive energies. Music has absorbed many to everyone's advantage, the vision-sound mix of the rock show coming naturally from working class cultural mores and oratory. Art Therapy has many others. Art Therapy appeals for it is putting art to use to aid humans in distress as well as the offer of that rare thing for artists. . . a salary, goddamit.

These occupations and others, worthy as they are in themselves, split and hide the massive strength of working class artists in this country.

We also become brilliant technicians for commerce, both in the field of Fine Art, by producing what the market needs (empty novelty with allusions to mysterious profundity) and in graphics and advertising. In Britain graphic and advertising artists are kept apart from the pure and authentic fine artists. Another barrier to the unity of artists.

Radical artists internalise these myths as much as anyone. People who work with advertising imagery are not considered proper artists and yet the skill and wit of their products is constantly admired. But within fine art it is common to find one group deriding another group as lacking in serious intention or whatever as they scramble for ever diminishing resources.

Human Creativity Obscured

When we are conceived and usually when we are born, we humans have all our faculties and everyone is inherently creative. It is only experiences of hurt that leave rigidities which even occlude some abilities and highlight others. Our creativity is never lost and can be recovered at any time by finding a healing resolution of these early hurt experiences.

IMAGINATION is not a separate area of the brain, nor is it something we have or have not got. Imagination is simply that type of thinking that reassembles memories of sense impressions into new forms. Imagination is a word that emphasises the sensory base of memory and thinking in contrast to language/symbol thinking which tends to be known as rational thought. These divisions tend to be thought of as real but they are simply systems of classifying thought which we have received from previous generations. Imaginations can also include rational thought and be guided by rational thought.

A friend who is in an executive position was talking about the integration of people with disabilities into mainstream schools. Essentially a basic human right.

She was wondering how on earth her daughter's class could manage if it suddenly had two blind people in it. I know a few people with disabilities and have often admired how they find solutions to the problems in their lives, given fairly basic resources, just like other people. I pointed out that the barrier to integration was in her imagination or rather thinking that the limits of one person's imagination represented real limits. So it happens that because a descision-making bureaucrat cannot imagine a solution it is assumed there is no solution. Whereas we could just as well assume that there is always at least one elegant solution to any social problem. And that this solution is most likely to be found by the people actually confronted with the problem on a daily basis.

Now I would say that such alienation of imagination in management has brought the socialist movement to its knees. Management and leadership must release peoples initiative not dampen it.

The Exploitation of Artists

Many of the objects required by the tiny and exclusive contemporary art market are posh consumer objects which have little use value in the production of meaning. The contemporary art market that buys works which fulfill this essential social function is even smaller.

People who make massive use of inventions of images and styles by artists, primarily the advertising industry, do not have to pay for this use.

There is a massive amount of paid workers living off art. Gallery curators, attendants, frame makers, glass manufacturers, auctioneers, critics, magazine and newspaper owners, TV programme makers, local and national arts bodies, publishers, administrators, technicians, tutors, so many people rely for their living on the artist who is paid next to nothing.

And art is defined as 'NOT WORK'. It's play, it's pleasure, it's fun, it's non-repetitive so it cannot be work.

Many artists are forced to be classified as unemployed. This poverty handout and the demoralising lifestyle that can go with it is chosen rather than giving up on their vision of self defined production. However it can lead to lack of self-worth, abjection and suicide.

For women artists the oppression is particularly acute as they have been systematically hidden from history and are now excluded from exhibitions even when women are selecting and names of artists are not shown. This shows how unconciously male orientated our concepts of quality are. And how these standards have been internalised by women as well as men.

The same WASP male standards also exclude artists of colour, working class artists and other oppressed groups. The idea that standards of art are absolute or universal and not culturally specific is a deeply imbedded classist myth.

Artists have attempted to produce work that in itself challenges injustice. The markets need for continual renewal of appearances feeds off all such innovation regardless of its makers intention. Without seriously and explicitly confronting the class nature of Art these individual rebels are easily contained and recuperated.

Liberation in art activity consists of attention to context and the initiation of new ways of working which emphasise the relations between artists, and between artists and people, rather than the previous emphasis on the form or content of individual work.

The Class Nature of the Art World

The definitions of art and artists are overwhelmed by upper middle class monoplies of the centres of power. The commercial and private galleries tend to lead trends and define what is shown in public galleries and what is shown as English art abroad to a greater extent. This in turn influences the policies of art education and publishers.

The art historical references that critics demand that good art be stuffed with are mainly owning class art history. The newspaper critics tend to review artists showing in a few mainly London galleries. Historians then use these public reviews...

As the sponsorship of art is privatised and inevitably comes under the control of the multi-national companies it is clear that their policies and vested interests will gradually mould the production of meaning and the construction of culture in the nineties.

On the other hand the trade unions' low regard for art means that they lose out themselves. For instance the massive T & GW has just one artist working on all their campaigns including the historic 35 hour week. It is incredible that the services of artists are valued so low when advertising is obviously so effective. By having this sort of attitude to its artists and therefore also to creativity, the traditional working class power base is cutting its own throat. This is another illustration of how oppressive myths & images are internalised by the working class and so seriously undermine its power.

"While we can speak of an advanced mode of production or a higher level of productive forces one cannot pass such qualitative judgement on aesthetics. It would be incorrect to say that African aesthetics are more advanced than European, or vice versa. There cannot be one correct aesthetic, nationally as well as internationally." *N.Kilele. Black Phoenix 2 '78.*

Multiculturalism often "lumps the 'values' and the 'assumptions' of working class culture, the ideas and interests which come out of the working class British, together with those that emerge from Britain's imperial history and high cultural artifacts." *Farrukh Dhondy quoted by C. Atkinson.*

In spite of these set backs it is becoming increasingly clear to all and sundry that Good Taste is increasingly in danger of itself becoming a quaint ethnic curio. Art retreats into obfuscation and esoteric post-modern theory. The confusions caused by this plethora of modern signifiers is an obvious defensive advantage to the uppercrust culture vultures and connoisseurs who can waffle about nothing and nod and wink to each other to their cognoscenti hearts delight. Enjoying the subtle interplay of conceptual light and shade of their own elegant aesthetic games whilst the new boys from the nether world of ordinary life are desperately trying to decipher the code and gain access to the glamorous world of wealth Within. Sign. "Only 2 children allowed in the sweetshop at any one time."

As we discard good taste and standards of excellence what do we put in its place ? Our own heritage is probably a wasteland smashed to oblivion by that very same Good Taste.

I would say don't worry about it. Communicate intent rather than window dress role. The rest will come. Aesthetics follows an integrity of action.

We are onto a new page... we will doubtless fail. But failure is an unavoidable part of learning new responses. The Culture of Success gave failure a bad press. But we know that there is more in the failure of an attempt at something important and difficult than the success at something easy, foolproof and of no consequence any way.

Anyway the pressure not to fail is a very adult thing which is quite contrary to creativity. Creativity is a lot of failure (enjoying every minute of the experiments!) and then finally the joy of success. And one persons success can be everybody's joy...

" one of the most insidious facets of British colonialism is cultural domination. When brute force and firepower established colonialism, cultural domination maintained it. When laws and institutions normalise repression, cultural domination reinforces it. When agitation and struggle threaten colonialism, cultural domination reasserts it. In short the cultural domination of Africans at home and abroad by Britain is an essential part of the political oppression of that one group by the other. Cultural domination is the process by which the culture and history of the victim is viciously devalued and eroded by the aggressor. Devalued to the extent that the victims no longer happily and willingly identify with their own culture and history. Devalued to the extent that the victims develop a belief that their own cultural identity is to be despised and rejected. The value system and culture of the oppressors become the value system and culture of the oppressed." *Eddie Chambers. Beyond Ethnic Arts, CIRCA 6.*

The Vital Role of Artists

Artists lead and define culture, cause peaceful renewal, picture human conditions and sensibilities so we can become more critically aware of them. Inspire people to think 'imaginatively'. The beauty latent in nature is realised in art. Quality of human experience is given relative value.

The value of something beyond monetary value is difficult to think about. We tend not to recognise such value unless it is emotionally charged or of obvious survival value (a mother's love.) The problem is that the linear and universal value system of money tends to dominate our thinking.

It is vital that artists gain a strong sense of the high value of their own work... to contradict the false messages of oppression. For this to happen as a social process, artists must support each other in generating this real picture of the value they produce, in contrast to the false picture of scarce resources which makes them compete against each other. Artists must take conscious responsibility to create social situations in which each person can gain a recognition of the value of their endevour.

The valuing of experience is an inherent characteristic of the human mind. As our senses take in information, the mind sorts out what is of value to us and stores it or offers it to consciousness for immediate consideration. As our memory builds a bank of these sense impressions we value each of them and compare and contrast new experiences with them to evaluate them.

The new experiences in turn may revalue the stored memories. This valuation and revaluation of experience is absolutely fundamental to our successful functioning and it is this process that art and play is all about.

This free play with value is how we sort out our choices and strategies for the future. Cultural adaptation on a big scale can require the creation of art on a big scale in a play with externally changing conditions. The extent to which a people are able to do this may determine whether or not they survive. This has been shown in the studies of the Cargo Cults of Polynesia. These people spontaneously created massive and highly imaginative rituals of adaptation to the sudden onslaught of western culture and technology. They would attempt to attract the silver birds which brought the westerners' magical cargo by making their own versions of western rituals such as cricket or airport building.

Art is therefore the necesssary mediation of value in our becoming. Only a free art of all the senses can articulate our future as whole human beings.

The apparent marginalisation of self-generated activity is utterly false. Our activity is in fact central to the integrity of our organism and the safe social development of our species. The work of an artist is as 'essential' as that of a postwoman, nurse or electrician.

"Artist Liberation is an important issue for everyone because what is at stake is the valuing of what is most focused and affirmative in the human spirit through the vehicle of artistic achievement.

"The artist is with every word, image, sound or gesture reclaiming and redefining human intelligence.

"The extent to which artists are devalued economically and in other ways is a reflection of a massive internalised feeling of worthlessness in the society as a whole." *Sally Potter, Letter, October 1985.*

52 GLAMOUR CARDS

A new form of an old

power game

Glamour is a TURN ON. . . Glamour is attractiveness incarnate. Glamour is the universal focus of desire. GLAMOUR IS HIGH TEC FASCISM.

☐ "HMMMM you are looking glamorous tonight." The associations are all positive and yet when we look past the glitz at what it is that glamour promotes, we see an ideology of elitism personified.

☐ The class system that dominates and is throttling the world requires a method to persuade us all to accept the scarcity of POWER AND BEAUTY, and that this is the natural order of things.

☐ Democratic ideals require that everyone should have a say. A dangerous idea that requires constant obfuscation. Glamour is distributed by chance amonst the population... every family stands a chance.

☐ These standards of glamour permeate the population with ever finer hierachies of good looks. Because of its apparent natural basis we all accept a position of relative superiority/ inferiority within this graded system. This order is constantly reinforced in the media.

☐ We accept the status given to us by our looks and at the same time we are taking on board the principle that a few people are SUPERIOR whilst most of us are INFERIOR.

☐ Glamour conditions us to accept the basic premise in which all class oppression is rooted.

☐ However we know that there is no rational basis for the valuing of one persons appearance ABOVE any other. That inherently everyone is COMPLETELY attractive and desirable. The fact that this rationally self evident concept is 'inconcievable' to most of us is a measure of how profoundly we have all been hurt by classism.

☐ Where did glamour come from ?

☐ The myth of the hero is ancient and almost universal. From people whose abilities seemed so far beyond mere mortals that they seemed like gods to the victor in battle surrounded in his glory. As a metaphor of overcoming, the hero has a deep resonance.

☐ The fair maiden and the handsome prince have long been a staple of western fairy tales.

☐ Western ideals of fairness have been an extravagant buttress to racism of all kinds. Gentlemen prefer blondes. Blonde-haired blue eyed children get adopted more easily. Blonde Barby dolls outsell black and red haired Barbys 10 to 1. Blondes get more attention and more harassment. Bimbos must be blond. If the product is up-market, use a brunette. The power of the myth is incredible considering its obvious banality.

☐ Myths of an ideal body. Crude old survival advantages of size are generalised and then misapplied to peoples' appearance. eg Penis and breast size irrationally equated with virility and fecundity.

☐ These ideals of beauty conflict with the reality of our wonderful physical range and diversity. Differences then seem significant divisions when in reality beneath the conditioning that makes us appear so 'different' human beings are 99% similar. There is an old fear of deviance and difference. Only complete normality is safe. As nobody is 'completely normal' the fear is active in everyone. Glamour is the idealisation of normality.

☐ One of the roots of the word is in the glamour or look that could entrance (a man). It represented the power of women. The reality of female power is now hidden behind a smoke screen of glamour girl mythology.

☐ Myth of invulnerabilty and protection from death. Ancient myths generated from an awe but also fear of death. Myths of heaven (perfection reached and experienced) and immortality.

☐ WWII was the first war in which carnage of civilians was a major aspect of the strategy. Over 45 million people died of which two thirds were civilians. The democratisation of war. Nothing on this scale or nature had happened before. This blanket legacy of terror paves the way for glamour. It is now understood how the experience of brutality leads to low self esteem. Glamour breeds on the demoralised and displaced.

☐ Glamour is a gigantic confidence trick in which we are manoeuvered into psychic self mutilation.

☐ Glamorising the role of men as warriors (Rocky is a top selling video in many parts of the world) prepares men for their continuing wholesale self-destruction in wars. The machismo of armed struggle makes it difficult to think of all the effective non-violent possibilities before resorting to such desperate measures.

☐ And yet although it appears to oppose death, Glamour is close to death because it is a mask. A shimmering picture of reality behind which is n o t h i n g. Living a glamorous life is a facade covering the most empty existence.

☐ Because glamour mythically opposes death and decay its ideal model of perfection is youth. The features of youth dictate many of the facets of glamour's criteria. Small snub noses, fair hair, smooth featureless skin, innocence. Picturing youth as a target of sexual lust inevitably encourages the sexual abuse of children.

☐ The glamorous are play-boys and girls. They don't work they just have exciting lives. As a little boy I understood the glamour girls would give me a good time (in contrast to the ordinary women in my life who as adults gave me a hard time).

☐ The recognition of parenting as actual productive labour is entirely contrary to capitalism, and the isolation of re productivity essential for its survival.

☐ The US is obsessed with childhood. Batman as a big adult hit film. It is selfconcious about its own youthful dominance as a nation. Glamour is the screen behind which Americans feel awful.

☐ Hollywood invented glamour. There is an oft quoted myth that anyone can make it in California, the land of opportunity. This may have been the case for some heavily armed whites in the pioneer days... but the reality now is of a massive class for whom there is no opportunity.

☐ It is the myth creation of the American owning class. It is the screen they hide behind. It does not represent the actual US owning class people who are as ordinary and common as any oppressors but is a mythical social ideal of superiority that is accessible, by good fortune to any family.

☐ American TV exports account for at least 75 per cent of all TV programming in distribution around the world. In some third world countries more than 80% of the broadcasting day is given over to U.S. reruns and U.S. multi-national advertising.

☐ Whilst the U.S. inundates the rest of the world with its own dumped TV exports, it imports virtually nothing...

☐ We strive for the glamorous ideals but there is nothing to be achieved. Glamour is Illusion. The only satisfaction to be gained from 'being glamorous' is that we are then NOT UGLY, not worthless. It is a sort of protection from feeling the accumulated shit of oppression which says that we are ugly and worthless unless we are rich, famous and attractive.

☐ Glamour gives the impression that beauty is not of the moment but fixed and consistent. To be a good glam model you have to have all round looks that don't fade or vary according to conditions, e.g.as you wake up in the morning after a hard night you've got to look just as beautiful. All of us are attractive when we are alive and animated. In spite of glamour we recognise this.

☐ The rules of this perfection are so rigid that no one can ever fulfil them. We are all 'not good enough.'

☐ Glamorous images include many real human characteristics, e.g. being vivacious or even simply alert. This conflation of irrational myth and human nature makes it confusing. Glamour really does seem desirable.

☐ These values are somehow very deeply held. It seems so natural to be attracted to a glamorous person. Of course being glamorous can give a person confidence in themselves (for instance) and someone confident is attractive. But even so, can we imagine changing our ideas of beauty so they are not exclusive ? Even the word exclusive has an alluring connotation. To me it feels very deeply natural but thinking about it tells me it must be false.

☐ No particular body type or human feature is intrinsically more attractive than any other. Such judgments are historically formed. Are artificial. Are culture specific. We tend to think of our standards of beauty as absolute and universal but in parts of West Africa, for instance, a high forehead and rolls of fat on the back of the neck signify those most attractive and beautiful.

☐ The fact these beliefs and values are so deeply held suggest that they are forced on us very early in our lives. And that concepts of desirable appearances are linked to the powerful motor of our developing identity & sexual values. For a very young person who is just becoming aware of hir SELF the information that we are not able to feel good about our identity/self unless we have a particular appearanceis a major trauma which it is difficult for us to imagine. If it had been simply information we would now given the arguments above be able to change our minds. However to me the values feel 'fixed'. Thoughts and values only become rigid when they are forced on us in a way that hurts or terrifies us. And this hurt does not have the chance for emotional healing. Therefore glamour is part of the damage caused to all of us by oppression. The earliness of this hurt gives us the impression that our judgement of beauty is something deeply innate.

☐ Apart from the original hurt of this perverted picture of beauty in the world, such pressure on people to have a particular type of body actually does accumulate and kill many people. Anorexics have lives dominated by physical appearance. Nearly all women are heavily pressured by issues of body weight and shape.

☐ Everybody 'knows' that it is part of the oppression of women especially; slimming clubs, schemes and foods are highly popular. Again rational 'health' reasons for wanting to lose weight can screen the oppressive functions. Instead we need relearning-to-love-our-bodies-as-they-are-clubs.

☐ Once the oppression is set up and internalised market forces create the demand to keep it in operation. The campaign for real people on the media is up against this. The picturing and participation of people with disabilities and physical differences in art and the media is a crucial part of all our liberation from the yoke of glamour. It can also be pushed through on a platform of equal opportunities. This is at present easier than trying to oppose glamour head on.

☐ Glamour leaves out the reality of ourselves as living organisms. As appearances we can take on a different sort of static existence.

☐ Body functions are taboo in the media... including birth and death (apart from violent death which is used as a symbol. The whole complex and profound process of death, dying and bereavement is rarely pictured). Such exclusions bolster the otherwise tenuous norm of glamour.

☐ A friend said "If only we could make socialism glamorous" This is typical of the confused thinking around glamour which stymies human development.

☐ Glam rock and now Vogueing make glamour IN-clusive and available for manipulation, deconstruction, having a laugh at. Generally camp culture has done some of the most liberating spoofs on glamour. Camp refuses to accept any natural basis for glamour. It is all reduced to an applied choice of bad taste. It converts glamour to Bad Taste from which position it is possible to reject it whilst retaining camp as a protective.

☐ Glamour ruins the relationships of people who aspire to its standards by putting impossible demands on their expectations of themselves and each other. Especially as they begin to age.

☐ People who have accepted that they are not glamorous are banned from the arena of first class life. They are never in the limelight.

☐ Only a human sense of humour about all this saves us from disastrous disconnection from reality. Fortunately glamour is pretty funny because it is so absurdly tragic.

☐ Glamorous people don't show or discharge fear (Except in highly dramatised situations). In fact they have the minimum of any emotional expression that might spoil their appearance.

☐ Because to be REALLY glamorous is to be The Complete Victim. The archetypes of glamour in their real lives will often become super victims. Monroe and Dean.

☐ Key requirements you need to fulfil to be a really glamourous person (rather than just look like one) is to be able to have natural facial expression, tone of voice and posture. Its important that glamour looks like the most natural thing in the world rather than the most fake.

☐ If your appearance approximates to a glamorous ideal you have the offer of advantage. It is difficult to ignore this offer. But if taken up it severly limits life activity such as care of young children. Nappies, grizzling babies, rough and tumbles, pillow-fights are not glamorous activities. Children never have media space being themselves. The glamour puss is not a mother.

☐ Glamour posits a life that is not tactile. Sex becomes a primarily visual activity. We come into physical contact only to provide ourselves with an exciting visual construction.

☐ The important everyday activities, relationships and struggle with our own situations past and present, are devalued by glamour as unheroic; not places for courage and dramatic music. In fact most of our struggles for liberation and most of the important relations in our lives happen here.

☐ Glamour is welded to consumerism and entertainment. Further discussion would require analysis of the alienated relations assumed by these concepts.

☐ People look more attractive on video. A dull thing looks better wrapped in cellophane. The body builders oil themselves and never touch each other. We describe one person as dull another as sparkling.

☐ Real life is pockmarked and frail and deeply satisfying. The media image of life is sanitised and glossy and dissappointing.

☐ The important thing in glamour is in defining power as NOT FOR EVERYONE but at the same time classless and arising from the masses by genetic fortune. The hierachies formed invade all human rela-

tions diverting our attention from our own real power.
☐ Oppression that is based on self exploitation and internalised negative images of ourselves is extremely unstable. And in real terms it is easy to liberate ourselves from it. The chains are in our own hearts and we have the key.

Other articles in this series on Glamour are to found in 'Collaborations', Working Press 1987; and 'Ruins of Glamour', Unpopular Books 1986.

HOLE/wHOLE 3,2,1.

In three sets of two these paintings by Stefan Szczelkun are copied from the before and after images used in the hair replacement adverts that appear regularly in the London Evening Standard. (see catalogue)

By elevating them into high art forms these bland oppressive images are called to answer for themselves. Bringing our invisible routine conditioning for judgement before the arbitrators of taste.

HOLE/wHOLE 3. The smallest pair are for first time buyers. They are quickly and guilelessly painted with no technique or regard for fidelity of proportion or territory. They are therefore without 'truth' or beauty. But for **£50** the pair who can complain. The naive blondness of youth.

HOLE/wHOLE 2. The middle pair are made with more painterly skill with the provincial dealer in mind. Perhaps a little dark and laden with history. Perhaps somewhat fussy in their brushstrokes. Trying neurotically hard to be serious oil paintings the HOLE is particularly disturbed. However it must be said that there is an attempt to relate the image to its context on the page and to the dimensional proportions of the original, but this is imperfectly achieved. A good investment nevertheless at **£500** the pair.

HOLE/wHOLE 1. The largest, and highest, are painted with the consumate ease, entirely self-confident skill and offhand spontaneity we would expect from a first class painter. In these two paintings the archetypes of oppressive polarity are perfected for their place in a national collection. Their attention to fidelity of scale is precise. Their relationship to the context of the newspaper page of their origin is standardised and brought under total control. 'HOLE' expresses the full vacancy and pain of 'lack' before its inevitable opposition in the replacement 'wHOLE'. Masculine dignity and virility is restored with bold blond strokes. **£5,000** the pair.

Szczelkun is not here taking the piss out of painting per se. The delimitation of conventional expression can go both ways. There is no liberation to be necessarily found in a switch to 'more radical' forms, media or styles. Or virtue to be gained by the non-aesthetic style of certain artists who have carved out a career niche for themselves as 'political'.

These pairs of heads are the limits of our common sense. We talk about socialism as its obsolescence becomes obvious on all sides. But who can foresee a social life and culture outside of money relations. The polar signs of arbitrary value fill up our heads like dustbins. The series of paintings demonstrate how the class system infests the roots of our thinking and feeling, polarising it in an arbitrary fashion.

HOLE/wHOLE 3.

HOLE/wHOLE 2.

1·36 M

HOLE/wHOLE 1.

1·36 M.

THE RETURN OF THE WRINKLIES

Glamour in the 90s

The following was originally printed in METRO RIQUET magazine No 6 (1989) which is produced in Paris by Francoise Duvivier. Francoise interviewed me about my book 'Collaborations' Working Press 1987 and this is an excerpt.

"I liked the articles about 'Glamour'. Our physical perfection is not only our main dream, we're looking for more and more a self controlled society without any emotions where moral and physical suffering, Death, too, are getting more taboo than before... And are you thinking that 'Glamour' comes only from any capitalistic society ?

"What we are saying is that the old myths of superiority/inferiority (coming from survival of the fittest??) coalesced in the cauldron of cinematic production to be reforged to serve the value systems of the expanding consumer society. White youth become the aspirant sign of Hollywood. The old who can appear forever young bear testimony to the 'reality' of this dream. Class society takes on a representative life that replaces heaven. We must aspire to the perfection of ideals of youth. We must oppose decay. Hide or gloss over putrefaction. It is the socially acceptable side of the fascist mentality. If 'fascist' can be taken to typify those who make superiority/inferiority as the nexus of their ideology. Gloss over violence. Or make it shock us into numbness. The new thing about glamour is its totality. Radicals all want glamour. Glamour is 'a good time'. Glamour is good sex. Glamour is attractiveness, life without a care. How can you oppose it ? If you deny glamour you cease to exist on the video screen of influence and power. Who wants to be real but insignificant? People that oppose glamour are a 'turn off' or dull. And yet the reality is that attending someone who is mortally ill in their last days could be a more profoundly valuable experience that any of the superficial hype of glamour. Childbirth is another example of an key experience around which we could derive cultural values. There are of course many others. Why do we waste so much time feeling empty desire or inferiority before the endlessly long legs of Glamour? Why can't we think in its presence?

We are all profoundly hurt by the systems of inferiority/superiority that plague the earth. They are not reality. Oppose them all and be ready for the emotional outbursts that follow any such successful action. They are an inevitable, and to be welcomed, precursor to change.

But even now (1988), as we begin to define our attack on glamour, its own internal contradictions may be rendering it a grist to the mill of capitalist renewal in the name of market expansion. I have recently received several reports on the FAX that say the yuppies' market has reached its plateau. Has finished its period of expansion. The advertising agency planners have been faced with startling statistics in their prognostications. There is an undeniable demographic shift in western countries as life expectancy soars and a large section of the mature population has accumulated capital and become a new consumer group, one destined to become a main area of flexible spending in ten to twenty years time. The creatives in the same agencies are facing a crisis; "How can we ever render the wrinklies attractive ?". An elders liberation movement could smack this marketing obsession with youth and glamour in the gob. Wrinklies still want sex. Wrinklies take drugs. As the rock and roll generation hits fifty five we can expect to see this demographic change in markets take interesting shapes.

But forewarned is forearmed.

LINES AND WRINKLES

SMOOTHED AWAY NATURALLY

Are you troubled by lines and wrinkles that are m-'-- you look older th--

The *II*

any long
easily be
Collagen
establish
correctiv
treatment
    Coll
which giv
suppleness
appearance.
process (w!
as 19!), you
fibres start:
becomes ur
outer layer
    In a s
procedure,
Collagen a
top layer (

The Collagen we implant
combines with your normal tissue
' -d smooth out your lines

nefits are
' you can
inger.
ve range of
edures for
des body,
ar re-
    Collagen
nd thread
it eyelash
ess
i-surgical
face.

THE

LON
BR'

Y
\TION
S

'UP

5494
'061
cepted

An original

Elblag 1989
▽

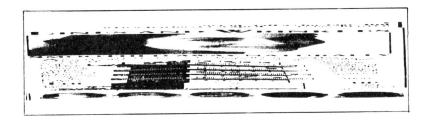

|—————————————————— 1·9 M ——————————————————|

△
Lodz 1990.

Stretched Blueprint

53

TOWARDS A WORKING CLASS ARCHITECTURE

Working class culture has always been devalued, debased and massively under-resourced. It is represented as cheap, vulgar, bawdy and without subtlety. It is designated into second class areas of culture like popular, folk and community art.

These areas are seen as lacking in serious intent and standards of excellence.

These are myths whose function is to oppress. They have no inherent validity. Yet they are internalised so thoroughly that they obtain the appearance of objective truth. Clearly a ballet is greater than a break dance. A cathedral is plainly greater than a garden shed. A liberated working class culture would be capable of things as great but they might look very different and be valued by completely different criteria.

The first thing that is required is the development of a critical conciousness.

Both of the existing dominant culture (making the ethnicity of the dominant culture clear and the ways in which this culture claims its superiority) and of the base activity from which all else is derived. An example of base activity is the ubiquitous garden and allotment shed. W/c culture has rarely been adequately resourced and so tends to exist on a small and or private scale where it involves the production of imagery (Myth production) and is usually only able to be expressed with commodity elements, e.g. Home decor. In this way the capability to produce imagery to challenge the status quo is curtailed.

Working class architects and intelligentsia have been conned into believing that they are a separate middle class. A lot of social archaeology needs to be done to unearth the rich and tangled mass of fragments which are the remnants of a tradition of working class culture, which is myth productive rather than based on consumption.

Here I examine a recent social phenomena in which there was a mass attempt to develop a modern vernacular architecture, an architecture which was ruthlessly suppressed with rhetoric and legislation. A lot of evidence survives to show how a working class architecture might begin to differ. If it had been nurtured, a completely different form of housing may have developed. A proletarian architecture could have evolved from these beginnings. Lack of cultural conciousness amongst the Labour party and Unions meant that these events went unresisted on an institutional levèl.

The development of British Shanty building relates to the growth of leisure. The shanties gave common people a free space to express more explicit their aspirations and identity. A space free of the restrictions of established traditions.

The first recorded attempt to impose work discipline was by John Crowley in 1700 in his iron works, demanding a 15 hour day starting at 5am and finishing at 8pm with 1¹₂ hours of breaks for breakfast and lunch.

Time discipline was seen as a Christian virtue.

During the 17th Century the modern 7 day week came into being punctuated by the sabbath. By the late 17th Century it became common in the urban manual trades to take Monday off as well. It became known as Saint Monday. By the 19th Century it was universal. This is the beginning of the week-end. By the beginning of the 19th Century the abstract concept of clock regulated time had replaced natural time. Time no longer passed but was spent.

It was not until the introduction of the Ten Hour Act and the factory act of 1850 which prevented juveniles being employed also on Saturday afternoon that free time became a possibility for the labouring people.

However the upper classes enjoyed much more leisure in direct relation to the wealth that they had accumulated. This led to the development of the holiday resorts in the begining of the 19th Century.

However surplus time was percolating down to the lower classes through individual initiative and through the class struggle to achieve better conditions. In 1871 the Bank Holiday Act was passed in favour of Banks only but soon it became general. In 1879 was the first recorded use of the word weekend.

Holiday taking was a general phenomena by the beginning of the 20th Century. i.e. taking time off out of the city. The first paid holiday for manual workers was in 1884 when Brunner-Mond gave their employees a paid holiday. By 1937 4 million people out of 18m

·earning £250 or less per year had paid holidays. Escape from the city was also made possible for the majority by the railway.

Shanties probably first arose as a response to the lack of resort accommodation cheap enough for working class people. Railway coaches that had become redundant were used as a basis for accommodation by 1900. Any existing well made container could become the basis of a shanty. These could be a fairground wagon, a shed, a nissen hut or a motor coach. Once the basic accommodation was there it could be added too at will. Enterprising landowners then got in on the act by renting or selling off small plots of land for building holidays huts on.

The Bungalow became a house form which symbolised leisure. Many shanties imitated this colonially derived ideal in their use of veranda. Colonial bungalows were also pre-fabricated and instantly erected on site. The logic of such instant housing must have appealed to the proletrian builders but few of them had the wherewithall for such kits.

Most shanties were built in the interwar building boom, particularly in the 30s, and before the 1947 planning act tightened up controls on outlandish development. Apparently the sprawl of shanty developments was influential in bringing this legislation into being...

"They constitute Englands' most disfiguring disease, having from sporadic beginnings now become our premier epidemic."

"Its intrusive impertinence knows no bounds."

Clough Williams Ellis. England and the Octopus 1928.

Ellis was a foremeost defender of the (rural) vernacular. This was typical of criticism from the cultural elite. It compares with what Cecil Sharp was doing with 'Folk music'. It can hardly be called criticism as these people were the apparently 'fair' spokespeople of cultural repression.

The first wave of legislation aimed at curbing the radical implications of this phenomena was the 1935 Health Act which gave Local Authorities the right to clear slum holidays settlements if they were considered a health hazard. But the lid was put on these developments by the 1947 planning act. The popular prejudice behind this is founded upon the mythical goal of home ownership which models the symbolic image of the house and neighbourhood. A home which is initially knocked up as a timber shed and added to as time and money allow is not something consistent with this ideal.

During the 30s an odd sequence of events caused the explosion of owner ocupied housing. (Investment in the Building Societies and the resultant speculative housing boom and easy mortgages followed the Rent Control act of 1915.) The ownership of a home therefor became a symbolic issue as social values coagulated around property ownership.

"Having no status as property and being a new building type created unselfconciously by people inexperienced as builders, there was an element of naivety in the appearance and siting of the shanties, the owners being unversed (or untainted) in the rules of convention." *P.Wren p.12.1982.*

The owned home is bought complete with a mortgage. The long loan repayment period requires a solid permanent structure. . . rather than adding to the house you have to keep up with the mortgage.

The shanties were an alternative way of producing housing that was less property orientated, less controlled, more expressive but which would not have been a generator of profit in the way that the speculative/ mortgage production dynamo has been. Therefore, rather than being encouraged to evolve, they were repressed in a way typical of any aspect of working class culture which gets to big for its boots. They were and still are a possible solution to housing shortages that developed spontaneously fron the working classes as a primarly celebration of their achievement of surplus time.

After '47 these demands were diverted to Holiday Camps and caravans. Some 50% of the caravans produced were never intended to move but the wheels gave them a loop hole through the planning act requirements.

I was interested to note on my recent visit to Poland that summer chalets built on allotments are very popular and clearly under less restrictions that they usually are in this country. (After the '26 general strike in this country workers evicted from their tied cottages often occupied shanty sheds on their allotments.) Because Poland was mostly destroyed by the War a lot of worker housing is very bland industrial blocks. People counter these concrete jungles with little weekend sheds which sometimes grow into miniture palaces surrounded by idyllic gardens.

Apparently such shanties are also common in Denmark and Germany and other parts of Europe.

What is the appeal of structures such as garden sheds and shanties? In spite of Ellis's propaganda they remain dear to our hearts. I would suggest this is because of the intimacy with which they are designed. Decisions as to where to place each element are made at leisure and obviously in touch with the materials. In addition the materials used, such as hardboard or bituminous felt, need regular maintenance for the structure to remain habitable. The whole ritual of maintenace encourages adaptation and expressive decoration. As the fabric degrades and is re-formed, it changes in a fluid way along with the needs of the user.

In contrast architects design on paper and at vastly reduced scale. Low maintenance and permanence are required to make the building profitable. It is however widely recognised that architectural design improves if longer is spent on design and drawings are worked up on the largest possible scale. As the shanties evolve over time they are imbued with a complexity and with the idiosyncrasies of their builder. They have a 'soulful' quality which is often lacking in professional architecture but which can be found in other spaces that evolve over time such as villages.

It does seem ridiculous that we have a 'housing shortage' when the working class is so capable of building housing for themselves given the slightest opportunity.

The research on leisure is lifted from a thesis produced at Hull School of Architecture. Holiday Shanties in Britain a history and analysis, by Phil Wren, 1981.

'24 Masterpieces'

DECONSTRUCTING THE CITY

Clearly the superiority/inferiority nexus at the heart of oppression has been part of our cultural formation at least since the misconception of class society several thousand years ago. The illusion of our powerlessness which grips us so completely is reinforced in the apparent inertia of our cities. Millions of tons of concrete, steel and glass towering above us in arrangements orchestrated by unseen hands with only the most perfunctory nod to democratic procedure, don't exactly inspire us to mould and reinvent our cities. Our heritage of the concept of NOT OURS is like a wet blanket over the rage of a class which labours on the building sites but never ends up with the fruit of that labour. Powerlessness has many gods, icons and mere mundane monuments.

To achieve a state of conscious evolution we must be able to reinvent our cities for our own pleasure and use. And shrug off these false myths of our powerlessness. Myths which claim a permanence of property relations as a basis of social stability. It seems a place where only art can really stir up the inert residue that has claimed our imaginative capacity to re-think our cities.

There follows three reports on large scale collaborative 'performance art' events which attempt to invent images and counter myths which might, like Trojan horses, sneak through the apparently impenetrable barrier of our powerlessness.

DANCE OF CRANES

The renewal of our cities is the largest scale productive activity of direct use to nearly all of us. In terms of the identity and quality it gives to the cities we inhabit it is of concern to all city dwellers. And yet we could hardly feel less involved. A new building appears and the assumption is that it has little to do with us. The decisions of what to build and where are taken by a financial elite that most of us have never met. We have come to assume it is "not our business"... something above our heads. But when it is pointed out, how could anything be so absurd; of course it is to do with us.

Planning laws and procedures have their good points and have had quite an effect on preserving a built heritage which could otherwise have been swept away for a fast buck. They can also be stifling in their suspicion of all change. The procedures by which the public are involved and consulted are dry and dull in the extreme. Few people are excited by such procedure, much less inspired. A paper board hung on a lamppost, a notice in the local newspaper. These are all we have to bring us alive to profound changes about to occur to our home environments. Things just happen... we've got used to it.

We need modern versions of traditional rituals. Events to engage our senses and involve our whole being in the larger meanings of what is going on. A full understanding of larger abstractions can only be achieved in a way that we can make use of if they are represented as symbols that we can absorb through our senses. And further these symbols must reflect in their relations to us and to each other the relations that the abstracts bear. To achieve this reification of abstract qualities and their relations is a job for the artist. In older times the primary abstract that concerned people was perhaps the turning of the year. But in modern times a more urgent renewal for us to consider is the renewal of our city environment.

Men build things. The biggest heaviest things that men make are buildings and their most impressive tool for doing this is the crane. This is generally 'men's work'. Women on the other hand produce babies. But what many people don't witness is an actual birth. Of course they know 'the facts of life' but this is somewhat academic compared with the dramatic reality of birth. This really struck me when I saw a film of a birth a couple of months before my son was born. I was to help at the birthing. I was shocked! I realised that it was the first time I'd ever seen a birth. At age 29 ! But it's not just the birth that is classified information. Everyday the TV is full of gore. The blood of people shot and maimed in fact and fiction. But we never see the positive blood flow of menstruation. Squirm. It's anti sexual. It's dirty. It's... well it's just blood actually. And yet it seems more feared than the blood of war. Why?

The result of these taboos is to keep men at the outskirts of the baby making process and to maintain women as sex objects. It also negates the value of these human processes of pro-creation. Parenting is unpaid work. And as money is the yard stick of social status and so to a large extent of self esteem, it is difficult to see this work as central and crucial. Paying attention to and playing with little children just doesn't sound half as important as building prestige skyscrapers. And yet of course it is just as important.

The building crane is named after the bird.

All migrating birds that arrive in spring to make their nests, mate, lay eggs and rear their young will be associated with the coming of spring. They are certainly a joyful sight and their return embodies hope and signals reassurance. For they indicate that the larger ecocycles that we are unable to be personally aware of are functioning stably. Bird flight in itself gives us a sense of freedom and sensuality that is not part of the mundane human experience.

Perhaps again it is self evident that the larger, longer legged wadding birds with their closer similarity to human form are more likely to awaken feelings of empathy . Whatever the reason, it is often these birds that are strongly mythologised by human societies.

In ancient Egypt it was the Ibis which was dedicated to Isis the moon Goddess, the enemy of all serpents. Troth escaped from Typhon disguised as an Ibis. (Troth was credited with inventing hieroglyphics) The Stork, Heron, Crane and Pelican then came to be protected by their similarity to the Ibis and 'shall not be eaten'. The entire Greek alphabet was said to be derived from the flight of cranes by the God Mercury.

In Europe it was the Stork which came in for special attention. Not surprising as it is one of the most fascinating of european birds, often choosing to live with humans by making its unruly nest on top of their chimneys. The males return from Africa first often to the same nest. Males greet returning females by throwing their heads back and making a clappering sound with their beaks. The offer to share a nest and mate is made with the offer of a twig. The nest is a great mass of sticks and twigs lined with rags, paper and any other available social detritus. The male looks after the nest during the day and the female during the night. Three weeks after hatching the young practice wing flapping, vigorously beating themselves into the air above the nest and hovering for several seconds. Young Storks were taken as models for human behaviour in their devotion to their parents. It was claimed that Storks could show gratitude and it was certainly believed that they brought all kinds of good luck but especially fecundity. In Poland it was enough for a woman to see a Stork in a neighbouring field to get pregnant.

They are essentially gregarious, migrating in huge well organised flocks of several thousand birds. The autumn migration is less obvious than their arrival in the spring because they fly higher. This works to emphasise their arrival as an affirmative event.

The Stork rarely appears in Britain and has not nested here since 1416 when a pair bred on St Giles Cathedral in Edinburgh. It is a measure of the tenacity of the image that this is still the most common euphemistic myth of human birth in this country. This popularity is not reflected in the contents of our national ornithological libraries which have no books on Storks. It seems there is no detailed study of the folklore of Storks in English. (Possibly something exists in German).

With their striking colour scheme, red beak and legs, white body with black tail, trailing wing feathers and eye patches they are dressed the part for such a symbolic bird. As a species they have been on the decline for centuries, however. With the threat to their wetland habitats and other modern dangers such as power transmission cables they are now an endangered species. This vulnerability of our favourite symbol of fecundity is an appropriate comment on a world in which the wealth brought by technology can be insensitive to the priceless and irrecoverable qualities of our earth's ecosystem.

Interestingly when I discussed this project with friends, Janice Booth reported that she had had dreams of babies crawling along the booms of cranes whilst she was pregnant. So if we could mix metaphors as in the dreams. . . babies and buildings . . . conflating the greatest products of men and women. As work they are both of great value, however different.

The metaphoric aim is to contrast the symbols and image of human birth with the symbols and image of large scale production. Whereas human birth is a taboo and private process centred on a woman, the equivalent birth of a building is a male dominated public activity. Steel cranes 'give birth' to production. They symbolise exclusion and power. To make a crane DANCE is to insist on the primacy of human value before economic values in production. To equate this invulnerable power machine of modern production with the Stork, whose existence as a species is threatened by the ecological effects of this machismo of production, is to alter the meaning of cranes in our cities. The relation of Stork to birth allows this mix to enter and restructure popular myth as a new cycle of meaning. As a whole the event will attempt to provide empowering images by mixing mutually exclusive metaphors.

This is my interest ...the intention of my art activity. Not to celebrate one company's building but to imbue the general potential of such symbols with positive meanings. I do not particularly wish to make a christening service for the big building of a very rich man. . . but I want to involve people in the buildings they will be using.

The symbols of birth mean also to begin again. There is, perhaps, always hope for humanity if we can remake such symbols afresh for ourselves.

Written with the aid of an award for research and development for Calouste Gulbenkian Foundation. At the time of going to press it has yet to be realised.

SCENARIO

Based on one person's journey from conception to birth.

Meeting at sunset . . . As people arrive one unlit crane is moving in segments of a circle. . . describing the hours of the day. The other presents objects to the audience. A shimmering fish, a house with a smoking chimney, a puppet giant, a car with its lights ablaze, a 50ft diameter inflatable ball. The cranes talk to each other. When the time crane has done twenty four hours it stops. (meeting 8 minute)

There is a haunting solo trumpet or bagpipe pibroch from high up in one of the cranes and a flock of homing pigeons are set free to wheel around as they orientate themselves. The cranes follow suite stoping at the four points of the compass as if to point the way to the pigeons. (courting 7 minutes)

When the pigeons are gone the cranes slew together in unison building up a momentum that is echoed in live music. Grand like a cross between cathedral organ and whale song it comes from the ground and speakers mounted on the tips of the crane jib. The crane structure is now lighted in sequences and smoke is emitted from the ends of the jib. Slides are projected onto the wall of an adjacent building of Storks in a natural habitat. (sex 10 minutes)

The cranes then stop and begin to oscillate in fan formation to frame an intense sequence of slides. Images of Stork myth & foetal development are mixed in with a sequence of single words. The music is complex and hectic. The musicians rise into the air on a hydraulic scissors lift platform. (conception 7 minutes)

Suddenly the cranes swing around together and come to a standstill. Waiting with lights pulsing. The slides repeat a key relation of word and image. The cranes swing into an infinity figure movement and many other lighting effects are turned on. There are then a series of scintillating and brilliant crescendos of light and sound.   (gestation 9 minutes)

At the height of this the cranes pause and a thousand pale balloons are released into the air. Filled with a mixture of air and helium they only rise slowly. Through this the newborn twins make their entrance in silver suits spinning from crane borne aerial connections. (birth & after 12 minutes)

The twins continue their aerial display backed up by dancers situated in the surrounding cityscape with torches. Darkness descends . . . the cranes are asleep but still flicker with inner activity. The musicians are busking on nearby street corners repeating snatches of earlier melodies. As the audience makes its way from the site they find they have to negotiate unexpected fountains of water.

'SKYLINE'

An account of a recent large scale event by ROU-TINE ART CO. using a specialised type of crane may be of interest...

A hydraulic beam was used to raise a small archetypal house structure over 50 feet into the air in a public event in Borough Market near to London Bridge on April 16th 1988. Visitors to a large concert at the adjacent Southwark Cathedral were intrigued. With its smoking chimney the house was clearly inhabited. At sunset a garden below the house, from which it had apparently parted company, was activated with fire as little hand-made books were thrown out of the house window to parachute down to the assembling audience. These books contained data and graphics derived from the five historical interest groups which architecturally dominate the site. Representatives of each institution then appeared with placards at various vantage points. They each protested loudly at this 'extravagent' art event, challenging the artist to explain himself. The house descended and a man appeared at the window apparently disturbed in the act of shaving. He gave a speech in reply, described by the next Evening Standard as neo Brechtian, which returned the challenge saying that perhaps the institutions which dominate this important site, the very birthplace of London, had lost sight of the ideals of their own formation.

" We need only raise up our heads high enough, we need only raise up our heads... not to allow our vision to be obscured by these monoliths of history that surround us."

The house ascended to its former position and minutes later the man burst through the roof waving a red silk flag and with white feathers streaming out from the hole to envelop the audience. The house until then lit by a powerful follow-spot had images of activity within a house projected onto it. The projection was then turned onto the cathedral with a stop frame film of a plant growing and dispersing seed. Plaintive whistles in the background played 'London Bridge is falling down' and a massive installation of smaller versions of the house on the skyline, clustered under the arch of the railway viaduct, suggested an abandoned village or memory which might be reinhabited.

This event challenged the effect that architectural monuments have in the metaphoric strata of meaning especially when they are in key positions, both spatially and historically. The history of the area was synthesised and encapsulated in a Quixotic image. A history that was not presented as overwhelmingly inert but one that could be challenged and changed. And as this was the 'birthplace of London' it obviously had broader implications. The use of books of knowledge from above was a neat satire on another myth which disempowers us... the authority of the printed word.

The use of cliche particularly with the house form and the use of red flag again challenged the way such inert monuments can also exist in symbols and language to block our fresh thinking. It was a wild, entertaining but above all incredibly ambitious project which was brought off in spite of the almost non existent budget for an event of this scale.(£500.) This was achieved by the collaboration of about 14 artists on minimal expenses and the donation of an aerial platform from EPL International. *Karen Eliot*

'Skyline' was part of an event called SITEWORKS organised by BOOKWORKS and funded by G.L.A. Routine Art Co. personnel included Helen Bowling, Philippa Haines, David Leister, Andy Allan, Cris Cheek, Jeni Briggs, Bambi, Andy & Penny, Jane Hartwell.

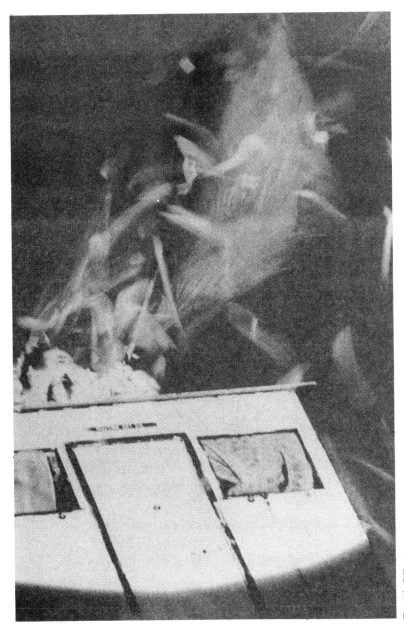

Patrick Gilbert

EMIGRATION RITUAL

Hull April 1989

In 1937 Hull had the largest fleet of deep sea fishing craft in the world bar none. The growth and wealth of modern Hull was based on this industry. The people who produced this wealth lived close about the docks in the Hessle Road area. It was a close community whose culture was forged in the drama of fishing life. The men would be away for 4 to 6 weeks at a time, sometimes only returning to land and their families for 24 hours before setting off again. The women in the community were powerful and self reliant. The recurrent tragedies at sea gave the community an intense shared experience which gave rise to a vibrant and distinctive culture.

When the fishing industry collapsed between 1973 and 1983 this community was suddenly deprived of its economic base. No thought was given to replacing this employment. The value of the community that had evolved was unrecognised. The solution from above was to get rid of the people from their slums and use this prime estuary site for development. People were scattered. Many were moved to the giant new overflow estates being built on the outskirt of Hull... Bransholme and Orchard Park.

Orchard Park was built in the early '70s to an apparently advanced design with an unprecedented two inside toilets and with an industrialised building system. It was mainly low rise terraces that were meant to reproduce traditional street patterns. From the start this half baked relocation without an economic base caused social problems. Problems that are now being addressed in various cosmetic ways.

Hull Time Based Arts, an artist run promotion group suggested I work on Orchard Park where they had built up some contacts. The commission had a budget of £750 all in. My initial idea was to get people on the eastate to build little houses on wheels and then make a journey back through their history with them. The idea was that nowadays there was no new world to emigrate to so we had to 'make the journey' as pioneers into our own history to locate points from which we could renew the present. It was to be a ritual aimed to fire people's imaginations rather than achieve change in itself.

The Workshops: The idea was enthusiastically received by a small group of residents who were keen to do something. I met them all individually and then we had a group meeting and briefly heard from each person where they had come from, which immediatley gave the group some homogenity. Wheeled trucks had proven too expensive but we had been offered the use of two all-terrain fork lift trucks so we decided to build the structures onto pallets.

There were four groups of builders, each with a different shaped pallet. Our building material was cheap sheathing ply which was to be stitched together with coarse string. As people started to consider how they would begin to make the walls, ideas came, and as the building progressed, continued to develop.

Debbie, Mandy and Debby decided to make a ship on their longer pallet. They asked for very little help and had a lot of laughs. Their committment and enthusiasm was central to the success of the project. We had decided that the builders could keep their structures after the event either for use in their own back garden as sheds or in a local school or nursery as play structures. This meant we didn't have to be too concious of the things as 'art'.

Gordon Brown, a retired construction worker made a conventional and beautifully detailed hut, which was quickly nick-named the swish chalet. This was decorated panel by panel by different classes in the local junior school.

Jim Scott, a Glasgewegian who had been a teacher and had lived for a while in Mozambique made a sort of political hut with help from Eddie. There were political jokes and slogans on the outside and inside on the back wall a tiny framed photo of the '26 May day demonstration in Glasgow. The inside side walls had colourful liberation posters from Mozambique.

Shelly Hickson and her family, with help from Mark Hudson, made a structure which evolved from a castle to a church and finally came to rest as the S & M CASTLE. The inside was fitted out with a range of manacles and 'torture' devices amid much hysterical giggling.

The amazing thing was that people had not only got sheds built in the four days but had produced a range of archetypes which accurately reflected their conditions. The ship being industry, the castle authority & oppression, Jim's house being peoples (past) struggle and the school house being the future.

The Journey: The sky was blue for the first time all week. We started off near the workshops. The idea was to stop, make an arrangement of the structures, take a formal photograph then move on to the next stop. This went OK for the first two stops on the estate but as we moved onto the public roads to go the few miles down to Hessle Road the slow speed of the fork lifts, plus the fact we had two forklifts for four sheds made progress frustratingly slow. To increase the tension we had to travel with the loads 'up', so the drivers could see, and this was illegal. On top of this we had technical problems with the large plate camera and the photographs were spoiled. Still we made it down to Hessle road and the huge forklifts driven by Jane and Thelma looked magnificent with their strange brightly coloured loads. We got our pictures in the paper and gave the ship a real champagne launch.

At the end of the afternoon the sheds were taken to the Posterngate Gallery where they were to be exhibited. On the walls of the gallery were a set of colour photographs of shanty houses by Dave Thomas, some large posters of previous Housework events done by me, photos and video from the journey, and work from the Orchard Park school. It all looked great and was appreciated by the builders who all came along to the opening.

The quality of the work done in four days was

amazing. Especially as we had just dropped in out of the blue. These structures will remain to remind people of this ritual to find new directions.

For 'Emigration Ritual' Routine Art Co. included Jim Scott, Gordon Brown, Mandy Lowe, Debbie Hickson, Debbie Jefferson, Shelly Hickson, Paul Hickson, children from Home School, Mark Hudson, Les Yorgensen, Tricia Maynard, Richard Merchant, Thelma Reynolds, Brian Precious, Rob Gawthrop, Frankie, Dave Elliss, Marion Grimes, Ben Mason, Tom Scott, Cath Shields, Andrew Smith, Bob Allison & Leo Hazlerigg, Jane Streeter, Michael Stubbs & H.T.B.A., Deborah Dean & Posterngate Gallery.

Bob Allison and Leo Hazlerigg